Evolving Woman
How to Thrive Thru Challenge & Change

Heather McDonald-Fercho
&
Raymond Aaron

ISBN: 978-1-77277-146-6

Published by
10-10-10 Publishing
Markham, Ontario
CANADA

Contents

Dedication

This book is dedicated to my mother. At a young age, her ambition was to become a teacher. Although her dream of teaching in a classroom did not come to pass, she taught me (and many others) life lessons that I can only describe as priceless. My mother taught me how to grow and care for plants, animals and people; the value of hard work; the pain of enduring loss and continuing to move forward; how to play the hand you are dealt and to understand that life may be unfair; but, to be grateful and to see the magic in every day we have. I hope to share her gentle strength and unbounding resilience with you.

Acknowledgements

Without Raymond Aaron, this book never would have made it to you. For me, it was sheer fate that I would be in the right place at the right time. I thank Raymond and his team for each part they touched in its making. From the conversations with Cynthia Trefry (who brought structure to my abstract thoughts) and guidance from Liz Ventrella, this was a group effort and will be a group success. Without this help and support, I would not have the opportunity to help you.

Many thanks to Brenda Malek Zahara for her editing help (over nips at Sal's in Winnipeg). She did her best to keep me on the straight and narrow.

I also want to thank all my readers who were kind enough to take time out from their schedules to read "Evolving Woman" and provide feedback. I appreciate their selflessness in helping my endeavour. Thank you to Brenda Malek Zahara, Eileen Hornick Wilmoth, Jane Hudson, Judy McDonald, Kyla Hunter, Colleen McDonald, Tara Gladun, Allison Coltin, Maureen McCoy Mateush, Nicole Olchowy, Debbie Cherniawsky, Winona Pidperyhora and Michelle Kelly. Special appreciation goes to Shauna Thompson who insisted on reading this piece while working through the emotions of having lost her family home to the Fort McMurray fire and the challenges of creating a new home.

Thank you to Dwight Elgert for lending his photographic talents to the outdoor shoot. Job well done!

Finally, I would like to thank my families, the family I was born into, the family I married into and the family I share all of my days with. I love you Andrew, Austin and Peyton.

Testimonials

Read Heather's book, *Evolving Woman: How to Thrive Thru Challenge & Change,* and feel her keen desire for every woman to realize and embrace their full potential. Read the eight chapters in one sitting and you will feel you have just experienced a personal seminar with the writer; share it with a group of ladies and experience a lively and soul-searching discussion; or better yet, read a chapter each day for a week. You will soon find yourself desiring to embrace your full potential!
Eileen Hornick Wilmoth, Williamsburg, Virginia

Impressive! I have had many of the same thoughts circling in my brain, but Heather has put them together into print with much clarity. This book is a great personal cheerleader, filled with positive encouragement. *Evolving Woman* is invaluable to individuals mired down by life's day-to-day challenges.
Jane Hudson, Tularosa, New Mexico

Pour yourself a glass of wine, or a cup of hot tea, and get ready for a book that will be as warming to your soul as a soft blanket. *Evolving Woman* is a panacea for every woman who is consumed by self-doubt. Heather dishes out common sense advice that, if taken to heart, can be life-changing.
Colleen McDonald, Winnipeg, Manitoba

Life can be overwhelming, especially for women as they move through the brave new world of feminism, workplace woes and family drama. The world seemingly only moves at lightning speed, and it takes someone like Heather to slow it down and make sense of it all. Reading *Evolving Woman* is like sitting down with a very smart, really calm best friend, who listens to all your problems and helps you sort them out. Easy to read, enlightening, and empowering, Heather's wise words will be a blessing to busy women who need assistance.

Kyla Hunter, Cold Lake, Alberta

Using witty analogies and relatable experiences, with a uniquely "female" perspective, this book challenges you to take an honest look at how your mindset, perceptions, and experiences shape your wellbeing, while offering tools and advice with moving to a place of contentment and self-kindness even through tough and turbulent times.

Tara Gladun, Calgary, Alberta

Evolving Woman: How to Thrive Thru Challenge & Change will speak to you in every stage of life, taking you on a journey of self-examination and empowerment. Heather gives you the tools to recognize your obstacles and teaches you to use mindfulness to overcome them. She inspires you to embrace and even seek out change, cheering you on every step of the way.

Allison Coltin, Thousand Oaks, California

Everyone needs to read this book. For me it is painfully honest and raw, but so very right and so very needed. At times, I was unsure to read the next line, being honest with myself about how much I needed it, was almost like admitting defeat. However, I would then feel overwhelming hope, learning something new about myself, and when I did, that I could be okay and will be okay. It was also difficult because it forced me to dig into years of buried stuff...

most recently dealing with my family losing everything to The Beast in Fort McMurray. No matter what you have dealt with or are dealing with, these words are as important to your well-being and recovery as breathing is to you being alive.

Shauna Thompson, Fort McMurray, Alberta

I found this book an enjoyable read. I could relate to many of the situations and I am a firm believer that you can be whatever you want to be with some hard work and belief in yourself. It is not always easy because others may want to keep you down. I found it inspirational and motivating!

Maureen McCoy Mateush, Winnipeg, Manitoba

With so much stress that we put on ourselves, especially as women to "have it all," it is wonderful to have the inspiration from another woman (who's been there), who is determined to help coach, inspire, uplift, and support other women rather than compete, compare and shame. Heather's words will encourage you to want to be better and to be part of the solution.

Nicole Olchowy, Calgary, Alberta

With the real-life experiences and vast amount of research, *Evolving Woman: How to Thrive Thru Challenge & Change* is sure to open your mind. This book is a thought-provoking, encouraging read that will help you to develop strategies to approach the challenges and changes in your life.

Judy McDonald, Stonewall, Manitoba

Heather's book came to me at a transitional time in my life. I had just lost my job with a company I had been with for over 15 years and I was dealing with a few of the emotions she discussed. I was able to put things in perspective and move forward confidently. *Evolving Woman* was written in such a way that I felt I was talking to Heather instead of just reading words off a page.

Debbie Cherniawsky, Calgary, Alberta

Heather's words really do embrace the women of today and how they may handle challenges and change. There were so many parts of this book I could personally relate to. Definitely a must read for all women going through changes in life.

Winona Pidperyhora, Calgary, Alberta

Evolving Woman: How to Thrive Thru Challenge & Change raises critical questions that every woman asks herself. Heather asks you to look within to capture the complexities of the female mind and use your uniqueness to help heal, set goals, adapt to change and grow positively. This book is for every woman who struggles with internal doubts, and provides positive exploration into how to harness a problem, and turn that problem into an opportunity.

Michelle Kelly, Calgary, Alberta

Foreword

Over the course of her life, Heather found herself getting stuck from time to time – and she is sure that you experience this in your life as well. It became apparent to her that you are often struggling through challenge and change in your life. You have the potential to be so much happier and more fulfilled than you are, yet you lack the courage or conviction to take the steps to become the person you wish to be. This realization lead Heather to action.

In *Evolving Woman: How to Thrive Thru Challenge & Change*, Heather shares what she has learned on her journey – so far. Her desire is that you understand and embrace the full scale of your potential. You are capable of accomplishing amazing endeavors, not only for your own gain, but also to benefit every life you touch. You should know that there is more than one solution for every problem, as Heather will teach you in her book. It is easy when you know how – so learn from Heather now!

Evolving Woman: How to Thrive Thru Challenge & Change emerged from ideas that came to her while holding conversations with others and researching how women's role in society continues to change. She has helped many women to manage their difficulties and can help you move forward with your life as well. She firmly believes that you, as a woman, can accomplish many things if you believe in yourself and are willing to work on yourself. She does not claim to be an expert, but a facilitator.

Heather McDonald-Fercho is an evolving woman. She credits the experience of growing up on a dairy farm for teaching her a strong work ethic, appreciation of nature, and resilience. Having worked in clothing retail, administrative jobs, hospitality, and management, she settled into one job for fifteen years. But the urge to grow and progress was ever-present, so she left that job after obtaining a certificate in Applied General Management and Professional Customer Relations. She later obtained real estate investment training along with studies in internet marketing. Her goal is to reach you, to help you overcome a challenging situation or inspire you to embrace a change in your life.

Loral Langemeier
Millionaire Maker

From Me to You ...

I have a gift for you. It is best described as a personal toolbox. In picking up this book, you have already identified something you want to change or a challenge you would like to overcome. Regardless of the type of problem you face or which strategy you decide will work in your situation, this is a 'blueprint' to get you to your next stage in life. Whether you need to rebuild your foundation, open sticky doors or windows to allow fresh air and light in, address major life renovation issues or something different, help is here. In this work, you will find support and options to work with while refining the next stage of who you are. I hope you find the comfort, encouragement and inspiration you need to get where you want to go.

Enjoy your gift,
Heather

Chapter 1

You Are Not Alone

"When the whole world is silent, even one voice becomes powerful."
— Malala Yousafzai

Change. As you read this book, you will hear me suggest a lot of changes to the way you have been living your life. Are you feeling uncomfortable? If so, something amazing is about to take place! The very word 'change' evokes different emotions in all of us, depending on the nature of the change. But it can be a defining moment in our lives. We often explain a situation and then detail how events take a corner and head off in an entirely different direction. But the degree of change may adjust our circumstances at a minor or major level. It may improve our situation or create a challenge. An improvement is greeted with relief and appreciation – who among us wouldn't enjoy good news?! Challenges can test us right down to our core, sometimes drawing out strength and resilience we never thought we had. Because challenges vary so much, it would be helpful to have a strategy to fall back on in times of need.

How are you today? You hear it every day from many different people. How do you respond? If you are like most people, it will depend on who is doing the asking. You may tell an acquaintance or business colleague, "Fine, thank you. And yourself?" If your employer greets you with the same question your response might be, "Busy, busy, busy." When your spouse or child asks, you could respond by replying "Ok. How was your day?" Different answers to the same question, all day long.

But, really, how are you? When you choose to answer this question superficially, you are setting yourself up to continually suffer in silence. The adage 'no news is good news' is false. No news indicates that you are suffering alone. Let's stop pretending that everything is fine. We all know that everyone is fighting their own private battle every day, so you have plenty of company. Why, then, are you pretending that everything is fine?

Most of us have been taught from childhood not to share what is going on in our lives. You may have been taught to keep your chin up and soldier on. You may hesitate out of fear of being labeled a complainer or whiner. You may not want to burden others with your struggles. Although this idea is admirable, it is ill-conceived. You tell yourself that everyone is busy with their own lives, and you do not want to bother them.

Chances are they would love to hear from you during a time of need. Think of it this way: Would you turn away from helping a good friend in need? You would probably bend over backwards to come to their aid, empathetically listening to their struggles while providing support and encouragement. A good friend would like nothing more than to give the same to you.

What would you gain by shutting everyone out and shutting yourself down? Absolutely nothing! The assumptions listed above that you may have considered as reasons why you would not want to "bother" anyone are not benefitting you or the people that care about you.. Just as you believe incorrect information, those around you are suffering from the same thing.

"No news is good news! She must have a lot on her plate. I'm sure I will hear from her when she has a minute. If there were something wrong, I'm sure she would call. She knows I'm always here for her."

Sound familiar? This is a phony cycle that yields artificial relationships. Continuing to isolate yourself will only compound and drag out the instigating problem while adding new problems to the mix. The longer you choose to sit in silence or answer with generalities, the sooner you will start to have more bad days than good days.

Reach out to friends and family for support. Let them know how you are truly feeling. Share not only the good, but also the bad. Be real with them. When you open yourself up to others, you allow them to open up to you. This is how authentic relationships evolve. You may never know the joy you bring to another by answering a simple "How are you?" truthfully.

After you have reached out for support, also reach out to find helpful resources. Do not tell yourself that this is too difficult a thing to do (there's negative thinking sneaking back in). Resources are all around you, and the means to access these resources are there as well. Reach up to seek counseling or higher education if these things will help you achieve your goals.

If you cannot pinpoint your problem, seek counseling so that a trained therapist can help you dig down to the core of what is holding you back. Sometimes our problems are rooted in childhood, and we need help finding them and weeding them out of our lives. Take advantage of the opportunities to grow and to be supported while doing so.

So, what is stopping you from embracing change? I'd wager a bet that what is stopping you, frankly, is YOU!. If you are living the typical, busy life of most women today, you are probably running on empty. Are you constantly stressed? Running frantically from one thing to another? Pestered by an endless to-do list? If you continue in this manner, you will be impacted physically, as well as mentally and emotionally. Being able to get a good night's rest will become next to impossible. Food will have no appeal, or it will become your band-aid. Either way, it is not good.

Quite often when a woman is living a stressful, sleep-deprived existence, she turns to caffeine or food to supply the energy and comfort she is dearly lacking. Stress can cause a loss of appetite, which takes away your enjoyment of the basic need to eat. Extreme loss of appetite due to stress makes eating an absolute chore that is like eating the blandest food for each and every meal. Who in the world would look forward to THAT?

On the flipside, just talking about foods you love can make your mouth water and conjure images of favorite meals. You may use food to lift your spirits or provide comfort at the end of a drawn-out, demanding day. It is no wonder that when you hear the term 'comfort food,' images and remembered smells fill your head, instantly transporting you to a safe time and place. You know exactly which foods make you feel better, at least for a little while. But comfort that is consumed does not last long. Food-based comfort may last a couple of hours or overnight, or it may only last until the meal is finished.

There are at least two issues that result from applying comfort food to your wounds. The first is unwanted weight gain, which is a slippery slope: "No problem. It's just a couple of pounds. I'll skip a few lattes and take the stairs at work, and they'll be gone in no time." The next morning you are running a few minutes late (probably from picking up the latte) and HAVE to use the elevator. But you will make up for it tomorrow, or the day after that, or the day after that. See how the problem is compounding? (No pun intended.)

If you are fortunate enough not to start gaining unwanted weight, the comfort food most likely is not providing the balanced diet we benefit from the most. Sweets, salty treats, and decadent morsels are all filling you up with empty calories and preventing you from getting the good food you need to nourish yourself properly. If you are malnourished, you are primed for depression and exhaustion.

Sleeplessness, overeating, and undereating can be three indicators to living in a constant state of stress. There are countless ways we attempt to make ourselves feel better during stressful times. You may self-medicate with recreational drugs or alcohol, which is extremely dangerous. Maybe you choose to drown yourself in work under the guise of getting ahead and making a good impression. Even exercise, something that is good for our bodies, can become unhealthy when taken to the extreme. Be aware of what you may be mindlessly doing that sabotages your health and well-being.

Another way you may be preventing change and growth to take place within your life is by limiting and berating yourself. Sound crazy? Stop for a minute and think about the voice inside your head that tells you who and what you are. Does it ever begin a sentence with a nasty , "Why did you do something so stupid?" That statement is the precursor to a session filled with brow beating and belittlement. Bullying yourself with negative thoughts is not only unproductive, but it is also mean. Don't be mean to yourself.

Now that you realize that you have may been creating obstacles that have you stuck in a place you do not wish to be, find out how to get "unstuck." First and foremost, stop beating yourself up! Hasn't that work been done? Are you not tired of constantly barraging yourself with negative thoughts? Put an end to it. Just as you extend kindness to your friends, loved ones and even strangers on the street, extend it to yourself. Put your foot down to the bully in your head. Send the bully packing and start loving and accepting yourself. Practice this daily, minute by minute if necessary until it becomes part of your awareness.

Once the negative thoughts have been cast aside, you are ready to replace them with a fair and honest assessment of your situation. What is going on? What are you really about? Are you happy? If not, what is stealing your joy? Reach out to friends and family and let them know what is troubling you. Be selective! Do not choose people who will focus on the negative; this will spiral you right back into beating yourself up. Rather, choose people who will give you an honest assessment in a kind manner. The friends and family you reach out to should be those who know you best, the good and the bad. You will not do yourself any favors by choosing someone who will only tell you what you want to hear. It may make you feel good for a while, but that feeling will soon go away, and you will not be any better off than when you started this journey.

So, where are you now in your journey through life? Stop. Back up. That was an authentic inquiry. Stop for a few moments, reflect, and jot down your thoughts. Where are you now in your journey through life? Was your reaction to that question positive or negative? Are you where you want to be? If the answer to that question is no, what do you want to change? Spend some time pondering the answers to these questions. This may feel a bit sticky and messy but stay with me. Remember, to get to where you want to be, you must become "unstuck" from where you are right now.

Many times, people blame their downward spiral on a loss of happiness. How many times have you heard, or said yourself, "I was happy until...." Or maybe you have heard/said, "When I have _____, I'll be happy!" Getting back to happy is a widely sought goal. If you were happy "until" an event occurred, that is a great indicator of where your struggle lies. Now, you will have to decide how to move forward; but, if you are waiting to BE happy, the wait ends anytime you choose. The happiness you are looking for is closer than you think.

When you hear the word happy, what do you think of? Does your mind conjure a fairy tale image of bright days filled with sunshine, bluebirds, and roses with no thorns? Happiness is not a constant state of bliss. Your feelings are wonderful things; they are a gift, truly. But don't let them mislead you.

True happiness comes when you learn to appreciate where you are right now. Appreciation does not mean complacency. If you do not like where you are right now, move forward!

When feelings are steering, you never know where you may end up. Your emotions change day to day, sometimes minute to minute! If you have a marvelous day where you have made significant progress towards your goals, and you are feeling on top of the world, do not think that you can sit back and stop working toward your goal. Enjoy the day for what it held and keep the memory of how you felt as a motivator to keep striving.

Conversely, if you find yourself having a bad day or going through a difficult situation, your feelings can overwhelm you as they wash over you in waves. You may feel lost, hopeless and completely powerless. Just because you feel these emotions, does not mean you are these emotions.

Rather than allow emotions to steer you, take control of them. Acknowledge how you feel in a given situation; recognize the feelings for what they are: enjoyment, irritation, happiness, sadness, elation, anger, etc. We have labeled some feelings as "good" and some as "bad." Feelings are neither good nor bad; rather they are indicators.

Quite often feelings indicate that we have a problem we are not addressing. Yes, even happiness can indicate that we have an unresolved issue. When the problem does not interfere with your day, you may end the day on a happy, high note. This does not mean you have successfully removed yourself from the problematic situation. It simply did not impact you on this day.

You are not alone. Every single one of us faces challenges throughout life. Change, especially unwanted change, is difficult for most people. Even desirable change is a struggle as it brings about life alterations. The tendency in our society is to put on a happy face and pretend that things are fine. Social graces dictate that we keep conversations polite and positive. However, there is a time and a place to be real and reach out for help. Now is the time. Reach out. Reach up.

As you read this book, curl up with a cup of tea or coffee and embrace these pages as a safe place to open up every corner of your life experience. Within these pages, you will find encouragement to take on the challenge or change you are struggling with. It is okay to not know how things will play out; you do not need to "know" right now, just trust yourself to be able to figure it out when the need arises, regardless of your particular circumstances.

Women endure so much, yet we often underestimate our strength. We heal from traumatic events but do not fully appreciate the capacity of our resilience. We foster hope for better things, even in the face of contrary incidents. This book is provided to create a toolbox of methods to help you along your journey. As you proceed down this path with me, I hope you will find the "best friend" that lives within you, and that you will discover that you are a part of the biggest support network in the world.

Chapter 2

Like a Moth to a Flame

"In everyone's life, at some time, our inner fire goes out. It is then burst into flame by an encounter with another human being. We should all be thankful for those people who rekindle the inner spirit."
— Albert Schweitzer

This book is about you. It is about all women. You may have noticed some chapters will look at what transpires within us, our feelings, reactions, and responses, during difficult situations. This chapter will examine a more removed element and its effect on women.

I do not know how we as women ended up where we did. Please do not misunderstand me; women have made great progress but there are still areas of concern that need to be addressed. Oddly enough, it seems the most progress is made in the face of the direst challenges. During the suffragette movement, in order to gain the right for women to vote, women were frequently imprisoned and beaten. But the right to vote was gained anyway.

During the second World War, women went from homes to factories and other jobs that needed to be done while their men went off to war. Many women paid the high price of these men who did not return. When the war was over, many women wanted to continue to work outside the home, and that want or need created new challenges for women.

During the days of the feminist movement, much of it sparked by Gloria Steinem, many women gained ground professionally and personally. Women living in developed countries may choose from a wide variety of occupations previously denied to them. We may lead global top money earning businesses or make discoveries worthy of the Nobel Peace Prize. Gratitude goes to all of the 'first' women who made these advancements possible.

The 'spark' for me was an article I read on the internet one morning. The article stated the sector expected to produce the highest number of successful entrepreneurs would emerge from women between 40 and 60 years of age. I was intrigued as the author explained how women were using these years in their lives to pursue and realize long held passions. Although it is frequently advised to choose your passion as your life's work, it may need time and planning to bring it into being. The author felt the women in the specified age window had time and other resources available to create their own enterprise. Some women may have held their business idea in their head or heart for many years. Others may have had the 'lightbulb moment' only recently and moved to action quickly. Regardless of the origin or the purpose, I believe every woman carries amazing potential to do and to be more than she is aware or currently sees in herself.

I seek to create a new perspective or paradigm for you. Until you are able to see the possibility, you are not able to move towards the outcome you dream of achieving. We are again in the early days of the next evolution of women. Much progress was made in the days of gaining the right to vote, in the initial days of joining the workforce, and during the creation and advancement of the feminist movement. To drive towards the next benchmark of progress, we need to be aware of some misconceptions about where we are currently.

Although there has been a push for many years to pay men and women equally for the same work, we haven't quite arrived. I would encourage you to advocate for yourself and for others who are doing the work and not receiving proper compensation. Stand up and be counted. The disparity in pay may range from 5% to a whopping 20%. Women are willing to accept lower pay in exchange for perceived job security, flexibility of schedule, or a shorter work week. (source: *3 Job Traits Women Value More Than Money* by Rick Janzen)

Here is a perspective you may not have been exposed to previously: As a man ages, his value increases, but for women our value begins to drop at a certain point, even though our knowledge and experience have increased. It is easier to show the difference in wages paid for services rendered and arrive at wage disparity. An abstract, or unconscious, social wall is more difficult to identify and combat. It may be as elusive as a shadow because the definition is more difficult to prove.

Case in point: Let's take a man and a woman of the same age and level of education and give them the same entry level job. Depending on their corporate structure, they may advance professionally at different rates. However, over time, men tend to advanced based on seniority, and their leader promoting them. This man is often attractive to younger females because he represents security and success. The male moves into the corner office, acquires a new, trophy wife (while discarding the wife and family who were there during his ladder-climbing years), and enjoys the fruits of his labor. On the other hand, women must work harder at the same job to prove their value. If women do not advocate for themselves, their advancement is slowed considerably, as are their earnings.

It is true that no one can take advantage of you unless you allow it to happen. We are seeing a newer trend for successful women to date and marry younger men as their male counterparts have done for decades.

I believe the perspective that women start to lose their value around the age of forty is obsolete programming for both sexes. When inspired to pursue what they love, women of any age move mountains. Having lived (and learned) for a number of years has hopefully allowed for some time to think along the way. Please understand that you will be happiest when you live your life as far and wide, deep and tall as you want. You are well able to do anything and everything, perhaps just not all at the same time. Understand, also, that choosing to work with and embrace change won't eliminate challenges. It will most likely create more challenges, simply due to the fact you are stretching more.

Switch your thinking at this point. Instead of employers asking what you can do for their workplace ask yourself: What do you want from your work? You may have held many jobs or had a different career or two and had mixed experiences at each of them. During the course of your work life, you have probably determined the elements you do or do not want in your next endeavor. If you have been paying attention, you have probably passed by countless opportunities and new possibilities for yourself. Any time you have become aware that there may be a way to 'build a better mousetrap' or a new way to advance an industry, perhaps it is your inner calling poking you in the brain. If you could choose a new path starting today, what would it be? If you have been working in a solitary setting, you may crave a more social atmosphere. If you have been overrun with 'people' issues for many years, perhaps less interaction appeals to you. Either way, you can build your criteria for your new future.

Make a list of things you do and do not want that will help shape your decision-making. Some women will decide to spend some time with family, or perhaps they'll travel before moving into their new role. That's great! Take all the time you need. This is the time to find your individual path. Right now (and for years to come), there is much to be done. If social issues are a passion for you, is it your time to run for public office or serve on a community board? If you have had an idea on the backburner for a product or service, is now the time to crank up the heat? Have you been yearning to return to school for some education to aid you in your next chapter? Do you feel a pull towards a certain group? Children? Elderly? Teens? Single parents? The more definition you bring to your criteria, the more fulfilling future you will create. So, what do you want?

Whatever it is…. go for it. Pursue that which gives you joy, using all the knowledge and resources available to you. If you find you need something you do not currently have, don't worry about it. Things have a way of working themselves out. Plan for the future, work in the present, hope for the best, and prepare for the worst.

If you take only one guiding principle from this book, take this: Anything life throws your way, you CAN and WILL figure out. Resourcefulness is your greatest tool.

Chapter 3

What's Your Problem?

"The truth will set you free, but first it will piss you off."
— Gloria Steinem

When you read the title of this chapter, you probably had many thoughts flit through your mind. Were those thoughts your actual problem or were they symptoms of your problem? Quite often we confuse our symptoms with our problems. Spend some time in self-reflection so that you can pinpoint your actual problem. You must understand the problem or you will keep coming back to it and will be unable to break the cycle. Regardless of what the problem is, we often make incorrect assessments.

Some problems occur in childhood and become such a part of who you are that you are not even aware that there is a problem. Conversely, you may have been chugging along, minding your own business, enjoying life when all of a sudden something went terribly wrong. It happens to everyone; although we all hope we will somehow escape dealing with a stressful, major life event.

When we do go through a difficult time, our stress levels increase and our bodies secrete higher levels of the hormone cortisol. Cortisol is the fight-or-flight hormone that causes your body to flood with adrenaline. If you are living in a constant state of stress, then you are always flooding your system with cortisol which can lower immunity and lead to health problems. This is not good. However, if you have a positive self-image, healthy coping skills and an optimistic outlook on life, the impact of stress on your immune system may be minimal. Attitude matters! This is excellent news because your attitude is 100% within your control.

Interestingly, there is more than just one kind of stress. Distress, something everyone is familiar with, is something with which you have probably had lots of personal experience. The flip side of distress is called eustress. Eustress raises the bar and challenges you to go farther than you ever have, confident you can do it! But let's look a little further into the distress side of things.

The Holmes and Rahe Stress Scale, compiled in 1967, gives a stress rating to life events. It is interesting to note that at least five of the top ten stressors often occur around middle age. This is the time in life when we may encounter the death of a parent or other close family member. We may find ourselves in the position of primary caregiver to an aging parent or in-law. This often occurs while we are also caring for our children or teens. At the same time, marriages often fall apart during this same period. Add to this a job loss or job change and this is most definitely a lot to deal with!

Let's explore some of the major stressors that can become problematic for us. All of these problems can cause low self-esteem that may last for years if you are unaware of the problem. As we explore these issues, consider ways in which you can begin to become "unstuck" from the problem or life-changing event. Even if the situation is not your particular problem, you glean some ideas for your specific circumstances. For every problem, there is more than one solution.

The ending of a relationship may be one of the more common life-changing events. Divorce is too common and not to be taken lightly. Often, when a relationship is coming to an end, and couples seek counseling, each wants to attend counseling in order for the other person to change. This is more backward thinking! Seek counseling to change yourself, not the other person. When a relationship ends, it is okay to ask why it ended. Do your relationship skills need work? Even if the current relationship is irreparable, you will be in a healthy place for a new relationship!

When a woman has an affair, she is considered a home-wrecker. When a man has an affair, the woman he had the affair with is considered a home-wrecker. Why is that? Your marriage contract is with your husband, not the woman he cheated with. He would be the home-wrecker if he chose to cheat on you. Relationships end when a couple focuses on blame. This is a waste of time! Each person must own their part of the relational breakdown.

You have a choice: fix the relationship or do not fix the relationship. If you choose to fix the relationship, take your focus off blame and put it on moving forward to repair the relationship. If the relationship is beyond repair, move on. Do not remain in an irreparable situation or you will be miserable. Again, spend some time in quiet introspection and counseling so that you can overcome the problems that the loss of a relationship holds.

Another loss that leads to problems is the loss of a job. This is an incredibly stressful event. Not only does the loss of a job bring financial stresses, but it is demoralizing as well. If a person remains unemployed for several months, she may become depressed. It is no easy feat to sell yourself to prospective employers when you are in a state of depression. Again, ask yourself why this loss occurred. If downsizing occurred, why were you let go and not someone else? Answering this painful question is the first step in finding closure on the lost job and moving on to the wonderful, new opportunity that is in store for you.

In addition to perfecting your resumé and seeking interviews, spend some of your down-time discovering what you would like your next career path to be. What would you like to spend your time doing? Do you want another job like the one you lost? Have you always wanted to open your own business?

Seek the skills you need to be able to obtain your new goals.

Sometimes we do not lose our job in the literal sense. Sometimes our job loses us. Do you feel that you have outgrown your current position? Have you reached the apex of your current career? Do you enjoy it? Has it become stagnant? You may keep the job you have and continue to plod along without stopping to acknowledge that you are quite unhappy or bored with it. You do not have to remain where you are. By all means, take classes, acquire new skills and get out of there! Job stagnation can lead us into complacency or, even worse, the idea that we are stuck where we are. Weigh your options and take action!

Another situation that can make us feel stuck occurs when we are struggling financially. Bills may pile up, and credit card balances rise as you feel a progressively greater loss of control. Money problems can certainly be overwhelming. There is a myriad of ways people end up in financial distress. Let's consider some ways to deal with this problem. The first thing to do is to get real about your spending versus your income. This is unpleasant because we like our stuff and are used to living at a certain level. Cut back where you need to cut back and make a plan to change your financial situation.

A problematic double-whammy can occur when people struggle financially due to a health crisis, whether it is you, your spouse, your child or another loved one who is ill. It is difficult to balance career and money when dealing with critical illness. Doctor's visits, expensive testing, costly medications and unpaid leave can compound financial distress.

Suffering from long-term illness or even a temporary health crisis will show the true colors of you and the people around you. Often, it is when we are going through our worst that people see our best; but, let's be real, there are some days when it is a struggle just to get out of bed when dealing with illness. A health scare rates pretty high on the list of stressful life situations, and it spawns other crises as well. I've mentioned the financial stress that can occur. There are emotional fears that can arise when faced with our own mortality or the mortality of a loved one. Emotional concerns present physical symptoms. Being unaware of the psychological basis of these physical symptoms may cause you to head down the wrong path looking for relief. All of these variables compound to add layers upon layers to the actual illness.

While we are suffering from a health scare, we often find ourselves surrounded by family. Some families bring out the best in each other and some bring out the worst. Either way, they know how to push our buttons! Families are filled with love/hate relationships. Some relationships with family members are toxic and can lead to all kinds of bad feelings. Even the best of familial relationships have strife from time to time. Family relationships are particularly tricky because these are relationships you have had your entire life.

 The idea that our families are inescapable and we must interact with them is false. Sometimes distance is a good choice as it can lessen harsh feelings. However, even when a person chooses to cut familial ties, they must work through the loss this brings. What was your part, if any, in the toxicity of the relationship? Why did you spend so many years steeped in a turbulent situation? Accepting that a relationship is unhealthy leads to self-reflection and, ultimately, self-discovery.

If distancing yourself from a toxic family member is impossible, learn to live a healthy lifestyle while surrounded by the negativity. Create boundaries and do not allow the hurtful family members to cross them. More importantly, do not let down your guard. A family member can only cross a boundary you have put in place if you allow them to.

The death of a loved one is the most painful loss a person will experience. There is absolute finality when someone dies. Grief consists of long periods of isolation, depression and loneliness. In fact, there are seven stages of grief a person experiences before the grief process is complete. Do not allow well-meaning friends and family to rush you through this process. Each person's journey is different. Allow the feelings and emotions to come, acknowledge them and know that they will pass. If you feel that you are "stuck" in grief, please seek help from a trained counselor.

These are just a few of life's situations you may have gone through, be living with now, or may face in the future. Whether you are currently going through one of these scenarios or not, you have your own unique set of circumstances. I hope that by reading about these situations that you have been able to recognize your problem. If you have not isolated your problem, maybe you have identified symptoms that you have been labeling as problems. This is a great step forward!

When you weed out your symptoms, you are more clearly able to define your actual problem. Once you have isolated the problem or the issue that is holding you back, you will be ready to address it. After your problem has been identified and a plan has been developed, your optimism and outlook will rise as your stress begins to slip away.

Here is a thought: Is your problem that you are creating problems for yourself? Do you beat yourself up and deny your accomplishments? When you are praised, do you feel that it is not deserved? Sometimes people feel that they are big phonies who are not really deserving of the accolades they receive from others. Does this sound familiar? Is so, you may have Imposter Syndrome. Yes, it is a real thing. The term was coined in the 1970's by psychologists who state that Imposter Syndrome occurs when people are unable to internalize their accomplishments. People who struggle with this syndrome feel inadequate and are plagued with chronic self-doubt, even when they are faced with evidence to the contrary. This is more common than you might think; over 70% of people have experienced these feelings at one time in their lives. (source: brightside.me)

Imagine that you have been working on a major project at your job. The project went fairly smoothly and was quite easy for you to complete. You receive positive input about your performance; however, you do not believe the praise because the project was pretty easy for you to do. Or, maybe you struggled with the project and just before giving up you made a lucky guess that turned out to be the right choice. You are praised by your superiors for your intelligence and performance. In this case, you feel that you do not deserve the praise because your success was based on a "lucky guess." You quickly dismiss the praise thinking that if someone else were to evaluate the situation, he may expose you as a fraud. This kind of stinking thinking leads to fear and self-doubt.

If you are troubled by chronic self-doubt, take heart because there are ways to overcome this kind of thinking. (source: brightside.me)

1. First and foremost, recognize that you are doing this.
2. Do not deny feedback and opinions from others. Embrace the accolades, internalize them, evaluate them objectively.
3. Do not attribute your successes to luck. You would not have been able to make that "lucky guess" without knowledge and keen decision-making skills.
4. Do not downplay your successes. You do not need to toot your own horn from the top of the tallest building, but you should be able to acknowledge your successes. You may do this in a humble manner without degrading the work you did.
5. Recognize that there is no such thing as constant perfection. Mistakes will happen. Evaluate them objectively, learn from them, and move on.

6. Recognize that it is sometimes wise to seek help from others.

7. Accept the fact that there are things that you do not know, there are things that you will never know and **there are things that you can decide to learn.**

8. While you are working your way through re-training your brain, keep a journal in which you list both your accomplishments and your failures. Be real with yourself and be objective. You will gain insight into these events after you've written about them. You will be able to look back over time at both your successes and your failures to see where you've been and where you are heading.

You are on your way! Move forward to reach your goals!

Chapter 4

Brutal Self-Worth

"We are born into greatness & conditioned into mediocrity."
— Unknown

Ever wonder about WHY you think the way you do? You have been taught to analyze, discern, examine and deduce by many people along your learning path. Lots of times we hear that our answers are right or wrong. There are at least two problems with the conclusion: 1) Perhaps the person asking the question is not aware there is more than one "right" answer and 2) Perhaps our 'wrong' answer becomes more acceptable based on the context of the question. Because others have 'never thought about doing it that way before,' they never thought of it as being acceptable. Their narrow definition of 'right' unintentionally limits the possibilities. This is their problem, not yours – keep thinking of those creative, out of the box solutions. Continue to innovate as only you can. So, is different good? Absolutely!

The world is full of all kinds of people who come in all shapes and colors with unique ideas and experiences. Why do we appreciate differences in others, but not in ourselves? Do you remember the Sesame Street song 'One of These Things (Is Not Like the Others)'? This song teaches children the important skill of comparing and contrasting to identify likenesses and differences. We often put this song into practice as we evaluate ourselves and others. Mostly, we have been trained to pick what does not fit.

Have you ever received a test back from a teacher then spent time poring over all of the questions you got right? Of course not! We focus on what we missed, not what we did well. This is our training! This is how our minds have been conditioned to process information. We are prone to complain rather than appreciate. In other words, we focus on what is wrong, rather than what is right. We focus on "red flags" as we essentially wait for a problem to arise, instead of being honed in on watching for an opportunity.

We need to change this mode of thinking where we focus on negativities. We must become the masters of our own barometers. To do this, we need to address low self-esteem. Quite often our image of ourselves is formed during childhood. Interestingly, we have a tendency to fixate on any negative ideas about ourselves that developed during those years and later years. Often we are too young and impressionable to question what we are told. Ultimately, a rotten foundation can be created. There are many sources from which these negative thoughts and feelings could have originated.

Most people's first interpersonal relationship was with their parents or other primary caretakers. Parent/child relationships are deep and multi-faceted. In addition to the many facets of this relationship, there are layers and layers of interactions, thoughts, feelings, memories, etc. Some of the experiences were negative since there is no such thing as a perfect family. You, undoubtedly, have spent a fair amount of time over the course of your life focusing on the negative experiences, since that is what you have been trained to do. It makes sense that if you were punished for negative behavior, but not rewarded for successes at an early age, you might have arrived at some pretty negative conclusions about yourself.

But parents are not the entirety of the community you grow up in. Next to parents, our siblings form our next longest, and often our strongest, relationships. We spend more time during our childhood with our siblings than we do with our parents. Sibling rivalry, at its most basic, is competition rooted in jealousy. Siblings compete for their parents' attention, time, favor, etc. They also compete for food, clothing, and toys, among other things. Many siblings grow out of these competitive feelings as they move into adulthood, but not all. Some people harbor feelings of anger or resentment towards a sibling long into adulthood. Other people continue to vie with their sibling(s) for their parents' attention long into adulthood, which can lead to strained relationships.

Other negative experiences occur at school. I am sure that you can recall a negative event that occurred while you were at school. Kids can be cruel to each other. Bullying is a hot topic in the news these days, but it has been around forever. Even if you were not bullied, you probably knew who the school bully was, and did your best to avoid him or her. Or, maybe you were the bully?

Maybe you had an encounter with an unkind teacher. Adults often do not realize how much influence they hold over children. A cutting remark or unkind word from a teacher can leave behind a deep wound. Furthermore, the experience may shape how you see yourself from that point on. Whether the remark has any validity is irrelevant; it has to do with what we fixate on and tell ourselves.

Perhaps you struggled academically. We internalize our perceived failures and begin to change our perception of ourselves over time. You may have felt that you were "stupid." You are not stupid at all. Every person has inherent strengths and challenges. Perhaps acquired learning, i.e. book smarts, has been tougher for you than for others. I promise you this: If you look inward you will find the talent you have. Hold onto it and make it your passion. When someone struggles academically, they become frustrated when they are continually unable to meet expectations.

Do you like to let people down? Know anyone who does? Probably not. How about getting up every morning believing you are going to let your parents and teachers down? Even the times where your day goes reasonably well, you probably downplay the good and emphasize whatever minor inconvenience popped up. This is one of the ways we have been conditioned into mediocrity. During childhood, these are the people you would most like to please. It is incredibly disheartening to struggle in this way; these conflicts can lead to anxiety, depression and anger.

People who struggle with learning disabilities or difficulties grow up thinking it is absolutely terrible to make a mistake. As a result, they stop putting themselves in situations where success is not 100% guaranteed. Often, people who have struggled with failure would rather lead a cautious life than take risks because of an ingrained fear of failure. Do you see how stifling this can be?

Other life experiences can impact how we view ourselves, as well. Occurrences during our college years or past jobs, as well as encounters with friends, extended family, co-workers, and romantic relationships, can all affect how we view ourselves. If you have ever been fired, think about how demoralizing it was for you. Initially, it may have seemed like you hit a brick wall. Whether it is a lost job or a lost relationship, the heart-wrenching rejection felt in the moment seems both numbing with shock, and then insurmountable. But as time passes, we pick ourselves up and move forward. We must learn to recognize that what we think about ourselves is often inaccurate and needs more analysis to be viewed fairly (and kindly).

How do you know what you know? When you are detailing what you believe you know about yourself, be willing to be open-minded. Try to see yourself through the eyes of someone who does not know you. What would they recognize in your interactions with others and what would they experience themselves? Is the information you currently have about yourself accurate?

After considering which information should be discarded and what should be refined, you will want to confirm your perspective by asking the following: What is your proof? Are you forming your opinions based on verifiable evidence or faulty information? This introspection may at times be difficult, but the process will create comfort in knowing yourself in a manner you have not previously experienced. The resulting personal confidence and new-found balance in making decisions that support the direction you are going are worth all the work invested.

Think of a $100 bill. Picture a crisp, brand new bill. How much is it worth? Obviously, one hundred dollars. Over time, the bill starts to show wear (just like you) but the value stays the same. It can be folded, crumpled, spilled on, washed and dried in the sun – still worth $100. As long as you have 51% of this bill (including the serial numbers), the bank will accept it as $100. You are worth STACKS of hundred dollar bills; more accurately, you are priceless. YOU determine your value - your value is not based on what other people think!

As you explore these areas, there will be a lot of self-discoveries that are not necessarily wrong but do need to be adjusted. Take care to keep and cultivate the grain of truth, and do not hesitate to discard the remainder that does not assist in your evolution. We have a tendency to be unreasonably harsh with ourselves. We may also jump to the wrong conclusions about other people's motives or behavior. It may be beneficial to prevent making a conclusion on why other people do what they do; mostly because we do not read minds. Similarly, take care to consider the sources when you view how other people see you. If the person has nothing positive to say about anyone, do not be surprised if they treat you the same. If they gossip about others or break confidences, do not be surprised if they do it to you! Careful consideration in your thought process will become your habit to be fair with yourself and others. This new grounding will be refreshing for your outlook! Enjoy!

Fear of failure is a huge contributor to low self-worth as it constricts and suffocates. Perhaps you are afraid to try new things. Or do you, knowingly or unknowingly, sabotage yourself so that you fail quickly with minimal ripples? What does failure mean to you? A failure to one person may be considered a great learning experience by another.

It is your choice how you choose to perceive failure. We all have our own benchmarks and life experiences that we use to determine what we define as success and what we define as failure. Please do not allow others to define success for you. Success means so many different things to each of us. We have already discussed how our past affects our present and can affect our future if we allow it to. How do we move beyond the past?

First, we must refine our perceptions. Begin by becoming mindful of your thoughts. Thought awareness is a valuable tool when you are trying to remove negative thinking from your life. Contrary self-worth may be so ingrained into your psyche that you are unaware of it. It may take time to become aware of these damaging thoughts, but try to be mentally present with your thoughts. Notice when you are particularly harsh with yourself. Allow these thoughts to come and go. Take note of them. As you become aware of your negative thinking tendencies, you will begin to see patterns that you can then address.

"Success is not final. Failure is not fatal" A failure is a dead-end only if you allow it to be. Failure is not the end of the world or evidence that you should give up. Rather, it is an opportunity for self-discovery. Spend some time investigating what events or choices led to the failure. Learn, learn, learn from your mistake and use that valuable information to grow and expand your horizons. There is always a chance that you will fail – do not run from it! Embrace it! You will have a much more gratifying future if you do.

Once you recognize how you got here, that is to say, you have found the root of your low self-esteem, you can begin to purge and fix. Get rid of the wrong information. This will likely require a lot of reminding as it is difficult to cull what we have always assumed to be true about ourselves. Start by studying less sensitive areas of your personal perception. Settle your feelings on smaller issues to build strength. When you are feeling somewhat fortified by your progress, slowly start to take on concerns of a somewhat larger matter. If you try to tackle the biggest issue first, it may yank the carpet out from under you, sending you for a nasty setback. As you reach your goals, these small achievements will boost your confidence and allow you to branch out to greater goals.

When you face a situation that would normally have you anticipating an adverse outcome, visualize it differently. Thinking positively may sound trite, but it can affect outcomes. If you visualize positive experiences your mood is lifted, and you greet the day or challenge with positive expectations.

Sometimes when we evaluate the 'worst case scenario' of a situation, we realize that it may not be the right path to take. Other times we realize that the worst possible outcome is not that bad and we make the choice to proceed. A good question to ask yourself is the acronym W.O.R.R.Y., courtesy of JT DeBolt, Will the Outcome Really Ruin You? Most often, the answer is no. In these cases, our confidence is boosted when we have a Plan B in the wings, just in case things do not work out. The key is to explore and evaluate outcomes rationally and plan accordingly.

You can now see how we have been conditioned into mediocrity, but how do you feel about being born into greatness? Brace yourself before you dig your toe in the dirt and mutter, "Aw shucks! Little ole me?" You are an amalgamation of every triumph and tragedy shared by the human race. And you are still here!

Let's return to the manner of thinking we had when we were new to the world. Suspend your disbelief and consider that all your current knowledge is outdated. Shifting conditions, both internal and external, may have completely reshaped the landscape without you noticing it. You have to reawaken your curiosity. Take nothing for granted. Do not substitute other people's opinion as fact. Check the information yourself. Grab your toolbox. Already, you are not the same person as when you started reading this book as your perception has already started reshaping. Have faith in your abilities. You will figure it all out on each leg of your journey. Be prepared to embrace your innate greatness!

Chapter 5

Toxic Relationships and Serving Vampires

"Don't compromise yourself. You are all you've got.
There is no yesterday, no tomorrow, it's all the same day."
— Janice Joplin

When you read the title of this chapter, you had someone pop into your head. Right? Who is your toxic relationship? Why do you have a relationship with this person? We tolerate toxic people in our lives; sometimes we spend years interacting with toxic people. Isn't it interesting that we will subject ourselves to toxicity, but we don't tolerate it occurring in other people's lives?

If your best friend was in a toxic relationship with a man, what would you do? Would you smile and pretend that you were happy for her? Or would you speak truthfully to her about the detrimental effects of her relationship? If her boyfriend belittled her in front of you, would you remain quiet or would you speak up? You wouldn't tolerate someone treating your best friend poorly, so why do you allow people to treat you badly? You have to be your own best friend and stand up for yourself.

After spending time with someone, ask yourself whether they were tonic or toxin. Did your time spent with them make you feel better or worse? Strive to surround yourself with people who make you feel good when you are with them. Spend less time around people who make you feel worse after spending time with them. Easier said than done, I realize, but make it a goal!

There are countless toxic behaviors that will harm you. I'd like to focus on the toxic behaviors that will deplete your spirit. These behaviors can be found within yourself or within others. Keep an eye out to see if you can spot these behaviors, either in yourself or those around you. You want to prevent negative behavior from getting to you and expanding.

Gossips: First, a warning about people in your life who gossip: if they speak negatively or break the confidence of others, how sure can you be that they will not betray you? Consider your opinion about gossip. What do you believe? What right do you have to discuss another person's life? And if you believe there is no harm in doing so, be prepared to experience the same behaviour towards you. If you choose to instigate or participate in gossip, think twice. Once a conversation moves from non-judgemental comments about someone and degrades into gossip, nothing positive is communicated. If all you are exchanging is negativity, how do you think that would affect your mindset? Interestingly, those most heavily invested in gossip are the most paranoid people you know & live or die based on who says what about them. Not something I care to engage in.

Worriers: I feel badly for those who allow worry to consume their energy. They invest so much emotion & time focused on the Chicken Little "sky is falling" mentality, it is a wonder they are able to accomplish much of anything. Worrying about what will happen next will drive you crazy if you allow it. Most of what people worry about will never come to pass & often would be outside of their control anyway. Resolve to dial down the worry chirping in your mind.

Dishonest people: I am reluctant to label someone as a liar based on the following observation. I found lying to be a conversation divider when I spoke with different family members & friends. Some people are of the mind that if someone lies to you (even once), it makes them a liar for life. Others feel that 'little white lies are okay because it may prevent someone's feelings from being hurt. Still another aspect is the person who tells a lie in order to protect themselves or others if they have done something on a level which may have serious repercussions. For me, the most confounding position happens when someone who you don't trust (based on past experience) tells you the unvarnished truth or someone you trust with your life lies to you. Therefore, I take all information at face value & wait for it to bear out, one way or the other.

Scorekeepers: These folks always have a running tally on who treats who better, who buys more expensive gifts, who does more favours for other people, etc. essentially turning life into some kind of contest. For all the scorekeepers out there - stop wasting your time & energy trying to 'earn' love, respect & acceptance. Be yourself and do what you feel you should do based on the unique relationship you have with each person in your life. If you are dealing with a scorekeeper, don't get into game playing with them. There is no upside to engaging in this contest.

Grudgeholders: Some people really have difficulty resolving issues with others & deciding how to move on with life. There is an old saying "Holding a grudge is like drinking poison & expecting the other person to die." A person who holds a grudge really ends up isolating themselves from others & allowing bitterness to govern their energy. Life is too short to waste precious time on grudges.

Narcissists: This person's attitude & behaviour has only recently come to my attention. These are the people who are always the hero of their own story. They have a sense of superiority over others & have a tendency to treat those they see as 'inferior' in a not so kind manner. They assume their perspective is correct & may be insulted if you voice a different opinion or disagree with them. Teasing a narcissist may often bring out their fangs & claws as they don't seem to have the ability to laugh at themselves & become furious at the idea of being embarrassed. Be careful around these superficial "Image is everything" people.

B.E.D. People: The final group I'm going to focus on are the blame (others), excuse (not my fault) and deny (what problem? It must be in your head) people. I have found people with one of these attitudes are quick to resort to the other two angles if they get hedged in by a situation. It is far more empowering to take responsibility and correct the issue than to deflect and allow the issue to continue. It's best to get out of B.E.D. and behave with more personal integrity.

Have you ever noticed that toxic people have a problem for every solution? These people are miserable and want you to be miserable with them. Spending time with consistently negative people may cause you to begin to see your life through a negative lens. This is toxic! You will notice that your outlook shifts downward, which may cause you to lose sight of your goals and dreams.

These people may subject you to emotional or physical abuse. Far too often, physical violence transpires between parent and child. Sadly, the strongest indicator of whether a person will become an abuser is whether they were raised in an abusive household during childhood. Children who are physically hurt or witness physical abuse may develop emotional and behavioral problems. They may become violent themselves. Or, they may gravitate towards a violent partner.

In adulthood, this situation may occur with a spouse or romantic partner. The instigator uses fear, intimidation, and physical violence in an attempt to control you. If you grew up in an abusive household, this might seem normal. If you did not, it might shock you at first. It is surprising how quickly someone will become accustomed to being abused. Physical abuse ranges from threats to murder.

A type of abuse that is much trickier to perceive is emotional abuse. Check in with your inner dialogue. What do you feel and hear? Do you feel numb, fearful, desperate? Are you filled with self-loathing? Do you blame yourself for your spouse's outbursts or snide, passive-aggressive comments? Emotional abuse can be verbal or nonverbal. At first glance, you may think "at least he does not hit me." If you are thinking this thought, you have just identified your problem from chapter 3. The scars and damage from emotional abuse may be much greater and deeper than those from a physically abusive relationship.

If you are in an abusive relationship, seek professional counseling. Your safety comes first. You should also be happy. No matter what others do to you, it is done TO you. You are not responsible for the way other people treat you, but you are responsible to get yourself away from abuse.

You have examined your personal problems and your self-worth. Consider your partner's self-worth for a moment; does he have low self-esteem? Maybe he is wildly successful on the outside, but struggles with feelings of low self-esteem and inadequacy on the inside. An emotional abuser usually has something or someone else to blame for their behavior. You may hear him say that he lashed out because he had a "bad day" or was dealing with a lot of stress. There is no excuse for abusive behavior. None.

Maybe your partner is not the abuser. Maybe your parents are emotionally abusive. This is a toxic relationship that, unlike physical abuse, carries over into adulthood. Do your parents constantly criticize your choices?

People treat you the way YOU let them treat you. There is no justification for emotional abuse. Again, please don't tolerate this behavior. It will be up to you to set clear boundaries with your parents to let them know what behavior you will and will not tolerate. Your parents may be unwilling to change, in which case you will need to decide how you will react to them. Everyone has buttons. For good or bad, parents know exactly where our buttons are because they are often the ones who put them in place.

If it becomes clear that your parents are unwilling to work with you, you may have to draw a hard boundary to eliminate contact for a while. Unfortunately, these are often the most difficult relationships to manage, especially if one of the emotional weapons used by your parents is guilt. This is a very complex problem with a very simple solution. Removing or reducing contact is a simple solution, but it is not easy to put into practice.

A situation that is a bit easier to deal with is an abusive work environment. I say it is easier to deal with than abusive spouses or parents because we are seldom as emotionally invested in our workplace as we are with our spouse or family members. It may seem impossible at this time, but you CAN find a different job.

Most of us have dealt with an abusive boss or co-worker. This is so commonplace that at least three movies have been made about it! First, there was 9 to 5 which came out in 1980; then Horrible Bosses hit the theaters in 2011 with a sequel in 2014. These movies were successful because people can relate to the abusive workplace mentality and they can find relief by laughing at the extreme antics of the employees in the films.

Our workplaces may be the most toxic environments we enter in our lifetimes! A toxic work environment has long-reaching effects as some tend to bring the negativity home with us. Additionally, it affects how we perceive our job performance, our productivity and ourselves as employees. No matter how trapped you may feel in your current job, you CAN make a change. It is not as impossible as it may seem.

Do you like going home each day? Or is your home life a source of toxicity? You do not have to be engaged in an abusive relationship to have a toxic home life. Maybe you are caring for an aging parent at home who is draining your strength and stamina. In this scenario, your parent is not toxic, but the situation may be. Do you go home to sullen teens who have left messes for you to clean up? Are you simply overwhelmed by the upkeep of your home?

These scenarios may cause toxic feelings, but you can do something about them. Maybe you need to hire a nurse to help care for your aging parent. You may need to establish some hard and fast routines for your teens to follow. Consider hiring a housekeeper to help you with the home workload. Do not allow a toxic home life to drain your energy. Do something about it!

Do you wake up each day and head out into the world in a stressed out state? Are you a nervous wreck most of the time? Does anxiety rule the day? If so, it is time to make a significant change. Find out what is causing you to harbor these toxic feelings and do something to improve your situation. We put so much effort into our outward appearance but spend little time focusing on the inside. People will focus their energy on what they can control on the outside because it is an easier fix than working on the more difficult inner areas.

Yes, it may seem impossible at first to cut ties with friends or family. It is not easy to alter commitments that have brought toxicity into your life. Finding a new job is a daunting task, but it can be done. Remember, to get to where you want to be, you must become "unstuck" from where you are right now. Seek the positive!

Toxic people are harmful, dangerous even. Perhaps you have people in your life who are not harmful, but they wear you down when you spend time with them. Pay attention to the people you spend time with and be aware of the effect they have. Is a relationship toxic or simply draining?

People who drain your energy are often referred to as "energy vampires." Again, someone you know came to mind when you read that. We all have that friend or relative who sucks the energy from us when we spend time with them. They constantly seek reassurance that makes spending time with them absolutely exhausting. A good indicator that you are engaging with an energy vampire is that you have a strong desire to take a nap once your encounter with them is over.

What do you do with this type of relationship? You want to be a good friend to the needy person, but at what point do you go from friend to enabler? How do you protect yourself in the process?

The first thing to do is learn to recognize an energy vampire when you see one. Their dramatic anecdotes may be engaging at first as you hang on every word of their theatrical stories. Or you may be drawn in by a hard-luck story and feel compassion for the person. Soon after you have become intertwined with this person, you may begin to realize that the relationship only goes one way.

For some people, the energy vampire is your spouse. Your husband may come home from work tired or stressed, expecting you to make him feel better. Of course, we want to help our spouse any way we can, but be mindful of whether the behavior is consistently draining. Do you feel tired, unappreciated, nagged, criticized or fearful of bringing up certain topics when you engage with your spouse? If so, there may be a vampire on the loose!

Maybe you have sweet, little vampires at home. Our children will drain our energy in a heartbeat if we allow them to. Make sure you set parameters so that you do not end up doing everything for your child. Many of the things we do for our children are habits that began when they were babies. Periodically reassess whether you should still be doing certain tasks for your child. In many instances, our children are ready and excited to take on new responsibilities.

Also, children need your time and energy, so make sure to set aside a significant amount of time to play with or engage with your children each day. Late night chat sessions with your teens are excellent opportunities to connect in ways that often get lost during the busyness of daily activities. This is not neediness or clinginess, but their earnest desire to interact with you. Quality time is essential!

Occasionally, our adult children zap our energy. They may visit for lengthy periods that leave us overtired. Or maybe you receive daily phone calls detailing every problem your adult child has faced that day. We love our children dearly, but we do need boundaries. It is okay to let the phone ring and to set a length-of-stay availability for their visits. Your time is valuable, and your children should respect it.

Long-term friendships change as years go by. Someone who has been a close friend for many years may suddenly become clingy and needy as your life changes. Say you move, get married, take a new job or move ahead in life in some way. Your friend may feel threatened by this and begin to pressure you to 'change back' into who you were before. She may start to cling to you and demand that you respond to calls or texts right away. She may become angry with you and accuse you of not valuing her friendship. Do not allow guilt to coerce you into dropping everything the moment your phone beeps with a text from your friend.

Do not get pulled into the drama of energy suckers. Energy vampires love to share their negativity with others; they feed off your energy. When you engage their negativity, you are feeding it and, believe me, it will grow. You cannot fix their problems. Do not be coerced into believing that you can.

It may become apparent that you need to pull the plug on a draining relationship.

Let's switch gears from toxic and draining to a tonic and revitalizing. Think about someone who makes you feel good after spending time with them. What feelings come to mind? Acceptance, comfort, camaraderie, belonging, friendship, understanding are a few words that come to mind when I think of my tonic relationships. These are the relationships that we all crave. When you find this kind of relationship, be mindful and put effort into building a mutually satisfying relationship.

"Be the change you wish to see in the world."

The above quote is a "bumper sticker" version of some of Gandhi's words. What he actually said is this: "If we could change ourselves, the tendencies in the world would also change. As a man changes his own nature, so does the attitude of the world change towards him…. We need not wait to see what others do."

Now this quote does not mean that you can change the world by changing yourself; however, you can affect those around you. If you show the behavior you would like to see in the world, others will take note, and you will notice that behavior coming back to you. Just as negativity begets negativity, positivity begets positivity. Be a tonic for others and you will find yourself surrounded by healthy, upbeat people.

I put this concept into practice, recently. I was in line at the grocery store when the young girl in front of me could not get her debit card to work. She was becoming flustered and panicked as this was the only method of payment that she had on hand. As I watched her dismay and embarrassment grow, I decided to help her, so I offered to pay for her groceries. The girl and the store clerk could not believe that I was willing to do this. The girl finally accepted my offer and told me that she would repay me. I quickly told her that I did not want financial repayment. I suggested that she could repay me by helping someone in need next time. I hope that I gave this young girl a new sense of awareness as to how she can step up to help someone in need.

Years ago I knew a waitress who had many loyal customers. Her customers were always happy to see her. Her goal in waitressing was to make sure that each of her customers felt better when they left the restaurant than they did when they came in. People chose to eat in that particular restaurant at a time when this waitress was on duty because she was a tonic for them. Her customers left the restaurant and went back into the world feeling happy and fed (physically and emotionally).

Reaching out to others can be quite simple. Try smiling at each person you pass on the street. Hold the door for people as you enter or leave a place of business. Thank people who do the same for you. These things are incredibly simple to do, yet you never know the difference it may make in an individual's life. Seek happiness by showing others that you are happy. It will come back to you.

Chapter 6

Catching Up

"The most effective way to do it, is to do it."
— Amelia Earhart

Are you playing catch-up? Or perhaps a current term may be 'operating in overwhelm'? Either way it simply boils down to feeling you have a great deal of things you need to get done and not enough time. As a woman, you are pulled in many different directions throughout the day: your boss needs your attention on an important matter, a colleague wants your advice, a subordinate has a question, your husband wants your attention, your child needs help with homework, your best friend wants to share her day, you have errands to run, and, of course, the laundry is piling up. You are a busy woman and catching up is always on the to-do list.

Playing catch-up can be frustrating and demoralizing, especially if you are re-entering the workforce after an absence, or changing your career path. Speak to any woman who pushed through the gauntlet in the process of upgrading or changing her area of work later in life. Be prepared to encounter stories you never imagined could happen. Handle with care! Use this information to expand your understanding, but do not allow it to defeat you.

You have gone through countless changes during your life. At the same time, employment has mirrored these constant changes. You are continuously forced to adapt to not only minor adjustments, but also complete overhauls in your work life. If you are unable to adjust, you may risk losing your job. Whether you have stayed home to raise your family or have been sidelined for other reasons, one thing is for sure: Change is not only inevitable but accelerating rapidly. You live in the Information Age. Available information doubles every eighteen months. This is not just the Information Age; it is also the Information Overload Age. Everywhere you go, your senses are assaulted by newsfeeds, marketing, music, and noise, noise, noise! Often there is no escape, and you just have to tune it out or tolerate it.

Employers are constantly under pressure to create the best financial results while cutting costs to the bone. Gone are the days of getting a job out of high school or university and staying with the same company until you head off into retirement in your "golden years." Forget the gold watch and pat on the back for a lifetime of dedicated service. Those times have been gone for a few decades.

Currently, the workforce may expect to have more than ten mini-careers throughout their employable lifetime. Ten! That is a lot of change! Combined with living longer and needing to work longer, that number could easily double or triple. The reasons for this vary. People find that they have outgrown their job, and they make a change. Or they may realize that they do not enjoy the career they went to college to train for, and they jump ship to a new endeavor. Women may switch career paths after having children. People see a fresh, new opportunity and go for it. Some people desire to be entrepreneurs and leave their careers to achieve that goal. There are only a few reasons why people change vocations.

Think about all the new procedures you have had to learn in the variety of jobs you have held. Did some of your co-workers choose to quit or end up being terminated because they were unwilling or unable to adapt to on-the-job changes? Many times new computer software may prove to be such a frustration and obstacle that workers will change the company they work for in favor of one that utilizes the application with which they are most knowledgeable. People seek that with which they are comfortable. If you do not keep up, you may find yourself obsolete.

Do not be afraid to explore these new horizons, especially if your employer offers to train you. Consider this: If your employer has offered training, the organization has a vested interest in your success. Intelligent employers continually refine their workforce to produce better results. One of the better results is no or low turnover, paired with current market expertise. Embrace the opportunity to expand your knowledge and experience. This will enhance your value to your workplace. Part of being an evolving woman is having the ability to accept change head on.

On-the-job training is also becoming harder and harder to find. Employers found that hires were receiving training at the corporation's expense, then moving to the same, but higher paying, position with a competitor. It became prudent for employers to screen for applicants who already possessed the needed training or education. This locked the revolving door and stemmed the bleeding of the training drain. So, if you are offered on-the-job training, jump on it!

For all the positions altered or lost, new jobs, careers, or business opportunities emerge. Take heart, there are loads of opportunities out there! Now is your time to step up and into the rest of your life. You just need some new tools for your journey. Do not allow yourself to become obsolete! Be the first to sign up for seminars, webinars, or trainings on new technology. Change is uncomfortable for most of us. It is different and requires effort and leads us into the unknown. Embrace the changes, regardless. The changes are coming, whether you like it or not, so you might as well give it a try!

As women, we deal with more interruptions to our lives and jobs than men do. Our roles change more often than men's roles do. We must continuously assess our futures and be prepared for change. Perhaps you are not interested in upgrading within your current field. So, climb the fence to a new field and see how you like it. What is stopping you? Eradicate those negative thoughts that creep in and go for it! A new field will require training, perhaps a new degree, or certification. Find classes and enroll. You will climb this fence one step at a time. Your best years are still ahead of you, no matter what your age!

Whatever your current position, you are NEVER "just a" _____. Fill in the blank with your current position, whether it is businesswoman, worker, wife, mother, daughter, caregiver, etc. No matter where you currently find yourself, there is always an opportunity for change. Perhaps you had your life path all planned out. Then real life happened, your plan did not work out and your path came to a dead end. The future may now look a bit murky, and you are unsure where to find your new path.

During your game of catch-up, you may have become depleted, worn out, and overwhelmed. This would definitely make trying something new more than a little daunting. All you have to do is take the first step. Do not worry so much about having the perfect plan. Toss the roadmap and step out! Big leaps are unnecessary, so take a tiny first step. The path will materialize; maybe only the next step will be known for a time, but it will materialize.

It has become more commonplace for women to continue to work much later into their senior years. Too frequently these additional work years are a monetary necessity, rather than the pursuit of personal satisfaction. Women are occasionally forced out of a long-term position due to a multitude of reasons. Often, they end up taking lower-paying jobs. Ladies, KEEP your options open and work towards a variety of employment possibilities going forward. These should be ongoing considerations: What do you want to do next? What will get you out of bed, excited to start the day? What will give you fulfillment at the end of the day? There are SO many options to choose from – how will you ever decide?

Take into account not only what you DO want, but also keep a list of what you DO NOT want. If you have been working in a solitary position, maybe being part of a team is a change you are seeking. If you have always been in a leadership role, perhaps you would benefit from taking a break from being in charge of others and should pursue working on your own. Weigh all the pros and cons. Your job satisfaction should be a contributing factor in this decision. Maybe you have a wealth of knowledge you wish to share with others. There are many avenues to arrange access to education, whether it be in person or online. Find your niche; deliver your message.

Have you been observant enough to find a neglected business sector or have a way to make a drastic improvement over a current business method? Female entrepreneurs succeed two-thirds of the time; men only succeed one-third of the time. Why is this? Men have been trained that having a back-up plan means you are planning to fail. They see this as a weakness and shy away from it. They tend to go all-in without considering contingencies. I believe women have a higher entrepreneurial success rate because women plan for the unexpected. We always have a back-up plan. Also, we tend to plan ahead by building up a nest egg of extra money for any future lean times.

I believe that women often adapt to career changes better than men because our roles change more often than men's roles change. A typical woman may go to college or be trained for a career, and then she gets married, and chooses to start a family. She will either stop working to stay home with her children for a time or alter her schedule to accommodate career and family. Many men can compartmentalize their days: At work, they think about work; at home, they think about family. Women have thousands of thoughts going on at any given moment. Our days are filled with constant change, so our lives are filled with constant changes. Women typically deal with more interruptions to their lives than men; therefore, they are used to interruptions, setbacks, or changes and may be better able to adapt to them.

One such change occurs when the day comes that your child(ren) graduates and moves away from home. Some children go on to higher education or enter the workforce by gaining full-time employment. Our children develop large social circles and friends may sometimes seem more important than family – at least, temporarily. You may feel that your kids do not "need" you as much as they did when they were younger. Newsflash! They will ALWAYS need you, but this is a great opportunity to re-engineer where you want to go in the next one, three, five years and beyond.

What better example would you be able to set for the people you care about the most than to keep growing personally and professionally right before their eyes? Seeing your possibilities, struggles, and progress would strengthen them to successfully manage change in their careers, personal transitions, and setbacks.

Consider the changes women had to make during World War II. This was obviously a time of monumental change for everyone; men, women, and children. Women's roles changed tremendously during this time! Women left their homes and entered the workforce for the first time. As the men fought abroad, women on the home front worked in defense plants and volunteered for war-related organizations, in addition to managing their households. When men left, women "became proficient cooks and housekeepers, managed the finances, learned to fix the car, worked in a defense plant, and wrote letters to their soldier husbands that were consistently upbeat." (Stephen Ambrose, D-Day, 488)

Additionally, nearly 350,000 American women served in uniform, both at home and abroad, volunteering for the Women's Army Auxiliary Corps. Women in uniform took office and clerical jobs in the armed forces. They also drove trucks, repaired airplanes, worked as laboratory technicians, rigged parachutes, served as radio operators, analyzed photographs, flew military aircraft across the country, test-flew newly repaired planes, and even trained anti-aircraft artillery gunners by acting as flying targets. (National WWII Museum). Wow! Women proved their mettle during this time and in doing so they served as excellent examples to their daughters and future generations.

Rosie the Riveter, along with thousands of women during the WWII era, serves as an exemplary role model to all women. We are no longer held back by gender roles or age limits. No matter what your age or current situation, your best years are still ahead! Today, women realize that they do not need to be afraid to reach for what they want.

The sky is the limit! Set your sites on what you want, roll up your sleeves and go for it!

Chapter 7

Unique Body Concerns for Women

"I wish that girls embraced their power and their worth and their value in their youth, and not sell it or barter it for anything and have to buy it back later in life. I wish for my daughter to grow up in a world where wonderful publications celebrate them for their originality, their individuality, their willingness to be true to themselves, and the courage to be scary and emotional to get shit done. I wish for women to stop apologizing for those very things that make us women."
— P!NK

Body image is quite a preoccupation for women. We tend to spend a great deal of time and energy thinking about our weight, or our appearance in general. Encouragement for women to focus on our body image is huge in our culture, and with this comes an equally vast potential for negative body image. Most of our thoughts about ourselves are not kind because we compare ourselves to models with perfectly airbrushed bodies. Women may encounter biological, environmental, social and psychological challenges related to gender, and these concerns can impact health and well-being.

The ideal female body type changes over time; whatever the ideal is at the moment, know that women everywhere are working hard to achieve it, or they are beating themselves up for being unable to do so. Why do we do this to ourselves? As women, we should band together and put an end to this kind of "stinking thinking" and learn to love ourselves as we are.

We allow external factors to contribute to the way we see ourselves. If body image is positive, there is a higher level of confidence and success. If body image is negative, it can lead to a lack of confidence, low self-esteem, and, in the worst cases, eating disorders. Unfortunately, body image can be formed from external sources, such as the media which often shows unattainable images. Being female in our society subjects you to pressures to be thin and beautiful, thin and fit, or thin and successful. Most women have struggled with weight concerns at some point in their lives, if not throughout their lives.

Our body image should come from inside us; the way we feel should come from within ourselves. We must learn to turn off the external commentary we hear from other people about how we look. Men, for the most part, seem more comfortable with themselves. If they're bald, they're bald. Men have learned to embrace themselves as they are; as a result, it has now become attractive to be bald. It no longer has a stigma.

Wouldn't it be wonderful if women also moved to a place where we were comfortable in our own skin? Do you feel 'less than' if you leave home without makeup or without your hair perfectly done? Why? Do not put yourself into such a small box. You will find yourself in the best place when you accept yourself.

Women compete with each other and dislike each other based on appearance. Why do we compete? We all want different things, so why fight? Choose to respond differently. Choose to feel safer when interacting with others. It starts with us. Don't just listen, but hear what others say. People will open up, and an authentic conversation will take place. What you present to the world is what comes back to you. We have the capacity to have entirely different experiences within our communities and to reach an entirely different collective experience based on how we treat ourselves and others.

Women have enough to deal with already without beating ourselves up over how we look. Being female comes with its own set of physical considerations. The inner workings of the female body are nothing short of amazing. As women, we begin to have unique issues with the onset of puberty that often follow us from our teenage years right through our golden years. These issues may start when we get the first period or need the first training bra. PMS symptoms range from mild to quite debilitating. How telling that menstruation has been nicknamed "the curse." And so it begins.

Young women who are first entering the workforce face different challenges than men face. During adolescence and young adulthood, women are often made to feel that they are little more than the sum of their parts. As they train to enter the workforce and begin to interview for positions, they may feel judged on their appearance, by men and by women. This would make anyone feel uncomfortable! Again, we must be comfortable with ourselves and know who we are on the inside.

For women who decide to have a family, pregnancy is a whole new ball of wax to take on. Some pregnancies are easy and others are extraordinarily difficult. Some mothers-to-be love every moment of pregnancy while others are sick the entire time and do not have the same outlook. From the early days of morning sickness, to copious weight gain and body changes, on to delivery, each person goes through a similar but markedly individual experience. Once the baby has been delivered, recovery begins. Many women suffer from postpartum depression, which makes the early days of motherhood particularly difficult. Then, there is the raising of said offspring.

Women often find it difficult to return to work after having children. During pregnancy, it is a good idea to explore your options. This is a good time to decide if you are going to return to your previous job or if you want to pursue something different that will allow more flexibility. Should you move in a different direction? Should you explore a new company? Put feelers out during pregnancy and let time serve you.

At this stage in life, your schedule revolves around your children even if you return to work. Your children and family come first, so you want to be in a place where you are able to accommodate them. If you return to your previous job, you may not enjoy it as much as you did before starting your family. You will be pulled in many different directions and want to make sure that you are personally fulfilled by what you are doing each day.

By the time the youngest is off to pursue secondary education, you will be older and wiser. You will also be getting closer to "the change of life." Women dread menopause because of tales of night sweats, hot flashes, irritability, and a host of other symptoms we have all heard about.

Menopause not only affects the body, but it also affects the mind. The constant change of hormones during this time can make you feel as though you are on a roller coaster. Your world may seem topsy-turvy, small issues that come up may seem insurmountable, you may cry at the drop of a hat, or you may find yourself screeching with anger. Every time your hormones change, your brain chemistry must adapt to the change. Sometimes the change occurs seamlessly; other times it wreaks havoc as it adjusts. Women also have a tendency to develop osteoporosis later in life, but that can be managed if you prepare for it and eat well or supplement accordingly.

Many women are looking for something new at this time in their lives. Is this a good time to pursue a new career? What do you want to do now? This is a time when you may be able to consider your wants rather than focusing solely on your needs. This may be a great time to pursue the things you have always wanted to do, but never had the time to pursue.

Aside from life's fairly predictable curve balls, we will now move to the "blindside" life events. One of those may be a breast cancer or ovarian cancer diagnosis. Breast cancer strikes women at younger ages than in past years. More and more women are being diagnosed with cancers before marriage or children. No matter when such an event happens, it changes the trajectory of your life. Having to deal with cancer or illness when you should be going to university, traveling, starting a career or family is an enormous challenge.

Body image comes into play when dealing with illness, as well. In Canada, only 15% of women choose reconstruction after mastectomy. It appears that older ladies are content with prosthetics. After facing the challenges and pain of the significant recovery from the initial cancer surgery, many choose not to go through another surgery and recovery. Is this an attitude of these women being happy with their bodies as they are?

There has also been a rise in ovarian cancer in recent years. Early detection is challenging for this cancer. For all types of ovarian cancer, the five-year relative survival is 45%. Women diagnosed when they are younger than sixty-five years old do better than older women. If ovarian cancer is found (and treated) before the cancer has spread outside the ovary, the five-year relative survival rate is 92%. However, only 15% of all ovarian cancers are found at this early stage. The five-year survival rate refers to the percentage of patients who live at least five years after their cancer is diagnosed. Of course, many people live much longer than five years (and even are cured). (source: www.cancer.org) The ovarian issue is internal, so you have no visible indicator. This cancer is just as devastating to your self-image, even though you do not see the devastation this cancer causes.

Cancer has a different influence on every life it touches. Depending on where you are in this journey, it may be helpful to keep a few ideas in mind. Cancer hits everyone in an individual manner. There isn't a "right" or "wrong" way to react or manage the challenges that come with this dreaded diagnosis. Whatever you are feeling, is what you are feeling; and there are no hard and fast rules for how you "should" feel. You have a lot on your plate to deal with in the face of treatment and recovery.

Being concerned with what other people may be thinking does not fit as a priority on your plate. Deciding whom to tell, when to tell them, and the amount of detail you wish to release is up to you. This is your life, and in order to give your all to getting better, eliminate any distractions you can. Surround yourself with the people prepared to "have your back" in this war. Because you ARE going to war.

One cancer survivor I spoke with shared with me the darkest thoughts she had following her diagnosis and treatment. She concluded that her feelings were of such a destructive nature, she might be judged as being a bad person. When she became aware that it was the events surrounding her that influenced her thinking at the time, she was able to disconnect from the shame and guilt she associated with the thoughts. She was then able to flush them from her mind and release the negativity she had been experiencing. So much less stress!

Sometimes, if the cancer is of a breast or ovarian nature, it may be fraught with additional emotions. Some women may feel diminished after undergoing a mastectomy and feel less physically appealing. Ovarian cancer statistics can be frightening because of the difficulty of detection and treatment or the inability to have a family after treatment. Because they are so many better resources for you to access than I can provide here, I would recommend seeking counselling in the specific cancer you are dealing with. You may choose individual counselling; if so, pay attention to the rapport between you and your counsellor. You may need to change practitioners if you don't "click" with them; it will make all the difference in your mindset and feelings of well-being.

Another blindside event is the unimaginable: rape. Just as being female has its assets, it also has a particular vulnerability. If you have been the victim of a sexual assault, please take in the empathy in these next few sentences. What happened to you is beyond terrible. YOU didn't do anything wrong. The person who inflicted the damage on you is the only person to blame. Whether it was someone you knew or a stranger does not make a difference. Often, women feel completely alone after a rape. The number of reported rapes each year does not come close to reflecting the number of actual rapes. Sexual violence is not an easy topic to discuss.

I hope the physical pain you felt during the attack has passed. However, the emotional pain may be with you for much longer. There are some emotions you may want to work towards letting go of, mostly because you shouldn't be carrying them. If you are feeling guilt or shame, you may want to seek professional counselling to understand the importance of disowning these toxic thoughts.

Rape is not a crime of love. It is a crime of anger, of control and of power. It does not help that the perpetrators walk around with a "concealed weapon" in their pants. Your value as a person does not change because of what someone evil did to you. Please don't shut yourself off from life and its beauty because of another person's hatred.

Our unique body concerns do not make us weaker. Sometimes we are not ourselves because of what we are physically going through. Take a step back, take a deep breath and say to yourself, "Normally this would not upset me; there is something else going on." Be aware. Use your feelings as an indicator to give yourself some attention. Treat the problem rather than putting a bandaid on the symptoms. Recognize when you are not yourself and set aside some time to take care of you. Women spend their lives taking care of others; we need to make ourselves a priority at times.

Isn't it interesting that people have the tendency to discuss the negative more than the positive? There are several reasons that we have a negative universal consciousness. First, people cling to their negative experiences. They embrace them and bring them out to re-live from time to time. This often happens during a low point as a person is feeling self-pity. Rather than eradicate the feelings of self-pity, people tend to dive in and wallow in past bad experiences. This gives those destructive thoughts a powerful foothold in your psyche.

Another reason for universal negativity is that people tend to absorb the negativity from others. The obvious solution is to spend time with upbeat, positive people. Also, you may need to ask yourself if you are one of the negative people.

So, how do you affect a positive self-image? First, eradicate the negative thoughts, memories, and people from your life. Next, surround yourself with people who love themselves as they are. The positive self-images of these women are contagious! Also, try this little experiment: Before you get out of bed each morning, tell yourself three positive things about yourself. These can be past deeds, good memories, current events, your body image – whatever positive thoughts you have. Do this daily and I predict you will naturally develop a more positive mindset. Over time, you will realize that you are living with a happy, affirmative viewpoint. Live your life with love.

Chapter 8

From Mud to Masterpiece

"We delight in the beauty of the butterfly, but rarely admit the changes it has gone through to achieve that beauty."
— Maya Angelou

Become comfortable with the idea that you will **always** be a work in progress. There are so many wonderful experiences, and events you can choose to engage in that will increase your sense of fulfillment. Be brave and seek out opportunities for growing your spirit. In some ways, revert to a younger version of yourself when life was simpler, and, in some ways, more satisfying. Remember what it was like to be excited to have a visit with a friend and just enjoy every minute? There was also a time when making a mistake was no big deal; it still isn't the end-all and be-all. Love yourself for having the courage and seeking out all the pleasures you deserve in life. But first, let's get rid of a little excess weight.

Now is the time to take a shower with a fire hose. What do I mean by this? Well, it is time to decide to get rid of the negative baggage you have stockpiled over time. Sometimes a simple shower will not be strong enough to remove the negativity you have accumulated over the years. You need to shower with a fire hose (or a sandblaster). You may need more than one shower, as well. That is okay. Use as many as you need. These dark elements cloak your inner spark so that it is unable to be seen by those around you. Flush out each and every dark element so that external light will reach your spirit and transform you.

Another analogy to consider is the act of moving. If you have lived in the same house for over forty years, you have a lot of stuff to sort through when you pack for the move. It is easier simply to pack everything up and move it with you. However, you now have fifty boxes taking up space in your new home that you never seem to get around to opening. When you do finally get around to going through the boxes, you find all kinds of things. You find things that excite you and bring back great memories – "Oh I forgot I had this!" You also have the boxes that make you wonder why in the world you decided to keep the items in it. You realize you do not need what is in that box, nor do you even like what is in that box.

We all have a lot of emotional baggage we do not need, either. This baggage should have been exorcised like a demon a long time ago. Now is the time to assess what you are going to get rid of and what you are going to keep. Start with a clean slate. People reinvent themselves all the time, and it is now your time for reinvention. Personal reinvention is similar to taking an amazing house or beautiful piece of furniture that has been beaten up over time and restoring it. We are going to bring back your original beauty. Stop hiding the beauty behind the negative baggage.

You do not have to open all fifty boxes today. Do it one box at a time. Take your time and be gentle with yourself. When you allow yourself to go slowly and gently, you will have an authentic experience. Some days you may open a box, peek inside, and then walk away. Other days you may purge three boxes. Afterward, take some time off, then tackle a few more. Do not hold on to anything you are not using or anything that is not good for you.

Are you beginning to be able to accept that you are a work in progress? The reality is that every person is a work in progress. Unfortunately, some people have decided to stop working. Others should not prevent you from working on yourself. Be patient with yourself. I know you want to reach the finish line, but the journey is a huge part of the process.

As you consider your reinvention, refine the way you talk to yourself. Instead of saying, "I'm not very good at ...." reshape that thought to, "I would like to be better at..." Then decide on the steps you are going to take to reach that goal. What do you want to do with this? You have unlimited potential and can do more than you realize. But you will not realize this potential unless you reach and stretch yourself. Reaching and stretching may be a bit uncomfortable in the beginning, but you have everything you need to do this right now. Do not say to yourself, "I can't because...." Reach. Stretch.

Take a moment to look back and revisit the eight steps to overcoming self-doubt, otherwise known as Imposter Syndrome. Have you been practicing these strategies? How are you doing? I hope that your perception of yourself and your accomplishments has changed dramatically! If you have not made as much progress as you would like, keep working! Real, lasting change occurs when you strive one day at a time towards the goal.

Do as much as you can to make progress and you will be surprised with what shows up to facilitate, to ease your journey. You will find amazing things in the most unlikely places. The work doesn't become easier; rather, you become stronger and better at working your way through your challenges.

Imagine having the ability to cocoon like a butterfly. Imagine taking all of the hurts and all that you want to heal into a protective vessel. When you enter the container, you are cut, bruised, broken, and torn. Like turning on a tap, fill the container with warm, healing waters. While you are in this vessel, you are surrounded by a buffer, allowing no further hurt to occur. As you immerse yourself in the protective shelter of your cocoon, the pain subsides and is slowly replaced by sensations of resilience and increasing strength. All that

61

you need absorbs through every pore. Everything that makes you the woman you want to be is surrounding you as you heal. You replenish from the inside. Once you emerge from the healing waters, everything within you will be healed. The old will be disappear down the drain. You are free to return to your safe pool anytime you need healing.

No one else can do this for you. Another person may make you feel better about yourself, but those feelings will be short-lived. You cannot depend on another person for your healing or happiness. Only you can do this for yourself because you are the only one who knows the depth of your feelings. Only you know what you have been through over the course of your life. Give yourself some credit. Think of all you have overcome, excelled at, and performed well on.

After you have completed the healing, or cocooning, process, find kindred spirits. Be consciously aware of what appeals to you in life; conversely, refrain from doing things you do not enjoy. If you are an energetic person, connect with people who do energetic things. If you are a low-key person, connect with people who enjoy low-key experiences. There are countless ways to invest time and energy in activities that you enjoy. You may wish to take a photography class, try out for a play, join a chess club, start your own book club...there are so many opportunities for involvement in areas that appeal to you! As you branch out and explore your passions, you will meet people along the way who encourage you to change for the better. These people are part of your journey. Make a conscious effort to spend time with people who make you a better person.

On the flipside of finding people you enjoy being around is to be a person that others want to be around. Becoming this person is time well invested because it leads to valuable life experience. If you see others who need help, help them. You are coming from a place of appreciation and abundance;

therefore, it is virtually automatic to help. If more people felt and acted this way, imagine the difference it would make in the world!

A diamond begins as a lump of coal. It will remain a lump of coal unless it is exposed to heat and pressure. Do you feel the heat? Do you feel the pressure? If yes, then know that you are being molded into something stronger. You are becoming a diamond. This process is uncomfortable as no one enjoys the feelings of heat and pressure. You may sometimes feel that you are in a pressure cooker and are about to explode. When the pressure mounts, step away and find a way to take time for something soothing. You must keep your sanity throughout this process of change. Keep your mind on the diamond you are becoming. This transformation is worth it.

There is a timeframe that begins around age forty when society, as a whole, looks at women as though their best years are behind them. I disagree with that! I think this is the best time. Female entrepreneurs have their best successes between ages forty and sixty because they pay attention, have a handle on the market, and do their research. Sadly, because they are fed false information about their value at that age, some do not make a move. Never substitute someone else's judgment for your own. Naysayers will say it cannot be done. If you listen to them, someone else will come along and do it because they know they can.

How daunting it must be, to be a pioneer who has a breakthrough and does something incredible! The Wright brothers are a great example. How much garbage and negative feedback did they have to put up with from those around them? They were probably told they were crazy. But they kept going, had a breakthrough, and achieved greatness. They had each other to lean on during this process. What about individuals who accomplish amazing things in the face of hearing it cannot be done? If we all listened to naysayers, we would still be sitting in caves, wearing furs, and eating cold, raw meat.

Congratulations! You have come a long way in a relatively short stretch. Give yourself credit for getting this far. Remember to celebrate the progress you make and cement the positive revisions you have created in your life. Now it is time to see yourself from angles that may not have been visible from your previous vantage point. You have sorted through an awful lot of life experiences to be able to uncover and develop a strong identity for the person you are becoming. So, where are you now?

Are you feeling more in touch with yourself? If you have not made the connection yet, it would be beneficial to retrace your steps. Maybe you left a few boxes unopened. Since you are going to start laying the foundation on which to build your masterpiece, pay particular attention to the corner you are about to turn. You need to be comfortable and confident in the strength and resilience of your base. To build your structure on a weak base is sure to result in a fragile house of cards instead of the idyllic fortress in which to house the treasures resting in you. You will figure this out. You are more resourceful than you realize.

By now you have shed a lot of excessive baggage that was weighing you down. You are peeling off the mud to find the beautiful masterpiece underneath. My hope for you is that you will incorporate mindfulness into your day-to-day life. When you are fully present and aware of how you are feeling, you are able to deal with negative feelings as they arise, rather than sliding into unhappiness. Remember the days when you went through your daily existence without questioning how you were feeling? No longer! Now that you have embraced desirable change, you are alert to assess your state of mind each day and remain on the path of a happy, beneficial life.

You are also mindful of recognizing and dealing with negative people and situations as they arise. This awareness means you will no longer remain mired in draining or toxic relationships. You have emerged from this process a person who seeks out positive, constructive people with whom you will spend your time. Hopefully, the negative people in your life will see the changes within you and seek the same for themselves!

Sometimes the most negative person in your life is yourself. Of all the processes you've learned in this book, the most difficult may be to overcome your internal monologue about yourself. Self-image is a mixed bag of information we take in from print media, movies, girlfriends, boyfriends, and even strangers on the street. Along with a preconceived self-image of what you 'should' be, you also experience countless mental and physical changes as you live your life. Be mindful that the experiences you've gone through have shaped you into the woman that you are. Embrace the change; embrace yourself.

Just as you are mindful of your internal monologue and the people you spend time with, you are also conscious of where you spend your time. Now that you have stopped playing catch-up, you are ready to begin taking steps towards achieving your goals. Gone are the days of trudging to a job you do not enjoy; you are equipped to seek out your passion and spend your days doing something you truly love.

My desire for you is that you have found encouragement to take on the challenge or change you were once struggling to embrace. You have developed a stronger faith in your abilities. You have realized that you do not need all the answers in order to facilitate change. You are ready to fly!

*"Everyone has inside of her a piece of good news. The good news is that **you don't know how great you can be!** How much you can love! What you can accomplish! And what your potential is!"*
– Anne Frank

www.ingramcontent.com/pod-product-compliance
Lightning Source LLC
Chambersburg PA
CBHW060556100426
42742CB00013B/2575